THE
PROJECT MANAGEMENT
POCKETBOOK

By Keith Posner & Mike Applegarth

Drawings by Phil Hailstone

"Project management requires a multitude of skills - from vision and planning, to monitoring, communication, leadership and, of course, delivery.

This pocketbook pulls together best practice from these diverse areas into one simple, easy-to-read booklet. Refreshingly, it has been written from a general business perspective (rather than I.T.), and is therefore applicable to anyone managing change."
Adrian Guttridge, Director, Andersen Consulting

D0958229

CONTENTS

INTRODUCTION 1
Who the book is for

WHAT IS A PROJECT? 3
Project definition, project
management cycle

SCOPING THE PROJECT 11
Setting objectives, SWOT, force-field
analysis and information gathering

PLANNING THE PROJECT 37
Considering options, 5 M analysis,
Gantt charts and PERT diagrams

IMPLEMENTING THE PLAN 67
Control point identification, the
participative approach,
communication, the change process

EVALUATING THE PROJECT 89
McKinsey's 7 S model, questions
to ask

PROJECTING WITH PEOPLE 95
Advice for a new project
leader/member, MORALE, selling
the benefits

FURTHER READING 107

WHO THIS BOOK IS FOR

This book is for you if you work in or manage a team to achieve an agreed objective.

Read this book if:

- You are involved in the management of tasks, such as accounts or personnel, where change takes place
- You wish to learn team skills and their complementary project management tools (it includes examples from projects the authors have worked on as leaders, advisors and members)

Armed with new skills, you will be able to:

- ✔ Identify each stage of a project
- ✔ Identify potential pitfalls
- ✔ Attend to the 'people needs'
- ✔ Use the correct tools at each stage

WHY THIS BOOK WAS WRITTEN

A few years ago, at a previous company, Keith Posner was asked to join a project team to review and downsize the branch structure. He had never been involved in a project of this size before. Having thought about it for a few seconds he said 'yes', and then thought: 'How do I manage the training and re-training of 1800 people?'.

He needed project management training but the only type available was IT based and no use to a humble HR manager! There were books but they concentrated on the process not the people. He felt he needed something that covered both, particularly as he was told 'people are our greatest asset!'.

There are, therefore, two areas which are covered by this book:

1. The **task** and the project management tools to overcome problems in any project.
2. The **people** and their roles, relationships and interaction.

Mike Applegarth worked with Keith on the project and together they discovered, after its 18 months' cycle, the importance of ensuring the team were 'on board'. This was as important as knowing which chart or project management tool to use. This experience led the authors to write a book that covers both hard project management skills and softer team skills.

WHAT IS A PROJECT?

DEFINITION OF PROJECT MANAGEMENT

The simplest definition of project management is:

> *'Managing a movement from one state to another'*

This could mean designing a rocket to fly to the moon or just the process of moving people and their equipment to a different part of the office or factory. It could also be the implementation of an appraisal system or a change to an accounting monthly report. The same tools and rules apply!

Each requires great skill and diplomacy and each is fraught with difficulties. There are also degrees of movement and resistance to that movement. This book will take you through the stages of a project to provide a positive outcome.

DRIVERS OF CHANGE

Why does a project arise in the first place? Usually because one of three 'drivers of change' has brought it about. These are:

1. Competitors force you to review what is currently on offer so as to remain competitive. Staying competitive means reduced costs which, in turn, means reduced overheads. This leads to the need for changes in the quality or quantity of resources.

2. Customer demands mean that the fastest and most reliable information must be made available, along with the widest range of products delivered at the lowest cost.

3. The intellectual capital of the organisation drives change as new ideas and products are thought up and used to develop new niche markets.

You may not have initiated the project but it has been assigned to you. **Therefore, check that your objective and outcomes are in line with the driving force behind the change.**

WHAT IS A PROJECT?

'TO PROJECT...'

A less simplistic approach is to refer to the dictionary, where it is no coincidence that the verb 'to project' has the following definitions:

- To propose or plan
- To throw forwards
- To transport in the imagination
- To make a prediction based on known data
- To cause (one's voice) to be heard clearly at a distance

All of the above are essential aspects of managing a project, only the scale of these activities will differ, not the activities themselves!

Hence, project management is really the co-ordination of a number of essential activities, which are being performed by other people. An orchestra needs a conductor: you will be that conductor – after all, someone has to face the music!

WHAT IS A PROJECT?

SPINNING PLATES

Comparing the project manager to a conductor of an orchestra is, perhaps, a false analogy. After all, in an orchestra every member is playing from the same music sheet, they already possess the skills to play the tune, and there's always the opportunity for rehearsals. Still, it gives us something to aspire to!

For those of a more 'reactive' persuasion the following would be more applicable:

Imagine you are spinning many plates on the end of poles. All you have to do is to keep all the plates spinning at once, or at least catch them when they drop!

To do this you need to share the vision of the project sponsors so that you can help them to realise their objective.

PROJECT MANAGEMENT CYCLE

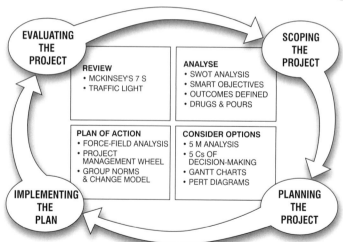

EVALUATING THE PROJECT

SCOPING THE PROJECT

REVIEW
- MCKINSEY'S 7 S
- TRAFFIC LIGHT

ANALYSE
- SWOT ANALYSIS
- SMART OBJECTIVES
- OUTCOMES DEFINED
- DRUGS & POURS

PLAN OF ACTION
- FORCE-FIELD ANALYSIS
- PROJECT MANAGEMENT WHEEL
- GROUP NORMS & CHANGE MODEL

CONSIDER OPTIONS
- 5 M ANALYSIS
- 5 Cs OF DECISION-MAKING
- GANTT CHARTS
- PERT DIAGRAMS

IMPLEMENTING THE PLAN

PLANNING THE PROJECT

PROJECT MANAGEMENT CYCLE

Planning is important to ensure that everything gets done and you are achieving your objectives or, in other words, that you are actively working towards your key results areas and not just reacting to situations as they arise.

By applying the project management cycle shown opposite and by writing down your findings at each stage, you can show the difference that you and the project are making, and keep the project in perspective.

This cycle provides the structure for the topics addressed in this book.

NOTES

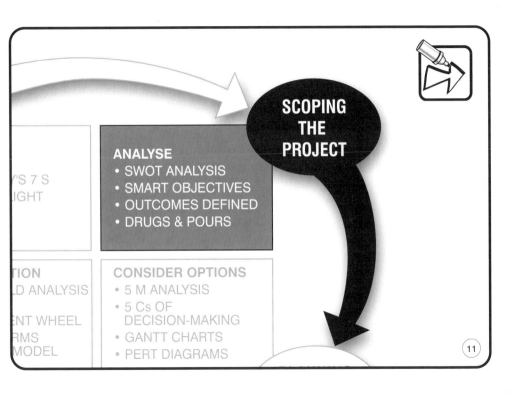

PROJECT MANAGEMENT CYCLE: STEP 1

Scoping the project is the first step once the project has been assigned, and is the point at which we prepare the ground. It is also the point from which things could go drastically wrong if it is not carried out properly. There is a tendency with many people to call meetings immediately to pull the plans together; yet, if the overall objective and outcomes are not defined and confirmed, all the effort involved in planning may be wasted. How often has 'they moved the goalposts' been used as an excuse when, in fact, they were never fixed in the right place to begin with? This step requires:

Setting objectives: collect facts, information, opinions, needs; question assumptions; define what's in and what's excluded.

SWOT analysis: **S** trengths

                     W eaknesses (present/internal situation)

                     O pportunities

                     T hreats (potential/external situation)

Design the strategy and identify key areas of work/skill/resource required.

DEFINING OUTCOMES & RESOURCES

Scoping is another way of identifying what 'the long and short' of a project is - what defines its completion and what range of activities it requires.

For example, what would be the scope of a gardening project where the lawn has to be presentable in readiness for a barbecue?

Firstly, we need to ask what it will look like when it's done well. Having defined the desired outcome, we then consider the resources required to achieve it. If the outcome were a lawn that wasn't scalped and where loose change would be clearly visible from three metres away, this could be achieved by using:

- scissors
- a scythe
- a strimmer
- a ride-on mower
- two rotary mowers working together, or
- a push mower

The factors we must also consider though are those of time, cost, quality and quantity. If time is no object and you have no money, then a pair of scissors could eventually do the job!

SETTING OBJECTIVES

Think about outcomes - what will the project look like when it's done well?
Decide what you want to achieve within a certain time period.
Think how the outcomes can be measured using the **SMART** test:

S pecific   Is the activity to which the objective relates clearly defined?

M easurable   Will the outcomes sought be visible when the project task is completed?

A chievable   Is the entire task, though challenging, physically possible?

R ewarding   How will the project benefit the organisation, team or individual?

T ime-bound   What is the deadline for completion?

Remember, if you haven't described the outcomes you will measure against, then you haven't done your job properly!

SETTING OBJECTIVES

EXAMPLE

Here's an example of a **SMART** application:

To redecorate the entire downstairs of your house so that:

- The walls, ceilings, doors and window-frames are cleanly finished in your chosen colours
- There are no paint stains on furniture, fixtures or fittings
- The carpet is not damaged
- The materials and labour costs are within budget
- No cracks or blemishes are visible
- The project is completed by 5.00 pm on Friday 13 November

Taking this example, would it be appropriate for you to criticise the decorators if they hadn't repainted the radiators and removed them to clean and paint the walls behind? Sometimes it is wrong to assume that contractors will do what is obviously professional!

THE 4 STAGES OF A PROJECT

1.
Set quality and quantity objectives

Ideas, problems and issues to resolve

2.
Plan and schedule time and cost

Feasibility of objective, specify outcome and plan everything you can

3.
Implement plan

Action; delivery of the outcome specified

4.
Evaluate results of the project

Take 'delivery' of project, correct any defects and learn lessons for next time (eg: What went well, what didn't go well and what would you change?)

THE OUTCOME APPROACH

An 'outcome' provides an objective measure that should not be open to misinterpretation. It removes subjective assessment and indicates clearly **all** the significant factors that determine success.

Quite simply, the project manager describes to the team members the **full** end result they will be assessed against before they get there. Contingency and 'what if' factors should be considered at the outset. For example:

- A sales manager is required to bring in £1 million of revenue; what if it costs him £500,000 in the process?

- A programmer is tasked with setting up a particular computer program by a set date; what if another program crashes as a result?

- A driver changes the car wheel and arrives safely at his destination; what if he had left the damaged wheel at the roadside or had damaged the car in the process?

Consider all the things you consciously look for but never openly express. **There should be no surprises for the team about what you are measuring!**

SWOT ANALYSIS

Use **SWOT** to identify the conflicts and forces at work, both internal and external.

You will need to establish how things are now (the current situation) and also where you want them to be by the end of the project.

It is often said by experienced project managers that whilst internal strengths and weaknesses do not tend to change rapidly, external opportunities come and go **but** threats usually remain.

SWOT ANALYSIS

Strengths/Weaknesses

These are always your own or your organisation's (internal) strengths and weaknesses. The following is a list of key aspects to consider:

- People/management expertise
- Facilities/building and equipment
- Technology
- Marketing/sales development skills
- Reputation/image
- Financial resources

Opportunities/Threats

External factors can cause your project to fail if you don't consider all the 'what ifs'. The following factors will affect how you approach the project, allowing you to be better informed at the planning stage:

- Political/social/economic changes
- Competition, locally or even nationally
- Market size and trends
- Profitability of market
- Needs that your products fulfil
- Likelihood of these needs changing

THE NATURE OF ANY PROJECT

No project is like another; there are different objectives, skills, people and resources available.

Since the advent of business process engineering, downsizing, etc, projects have had to come up with quicker, more effective solutions to problems. For instance, all of us have to reduce the time a product takes to get to market or speed up the response time to customers.

As a basis for information gathering think **SQID** when approaching any project. See, for example, how it applies to acquiring a new computer system:

S peed of response to customer enquiries and requirements
How quickly do we need the computer system? How will it speed up our service?

Q uality of product and advice
Why do we want the new system? What must it be able to do? What must it be compatible with?

I nformation must be able to be fed in and should cross traditional functional boundaries without difficulties
Will we be able to use the new system the moment it arrives? What are the consequences of mistakes being made during the changeover? How are the desired outcomes expressed to the contractor?

D elivery time to the customer or to the next link in the supply chain must be the shortest necessary to complete the job
Is there a learning curve to experience and, if so, for how long? If we use a contractor to set us up, when could the job be done and what support will be available?

SCOPING MEASURES
EXAMPLE

Imagine a project where you and three colleagues have to deliver a sales presentation in Brussels. How will you go about it, bearing in mind constraints of time, cost, quality and quantity?

Travel
- Clearly, you can go to Brussels from London by many means.
- If time is no object, then walk or go by bike.
- If money is not constrained, go by Eurostar train, first class, or by plane.
- If you need to work during travel time, then take the train or ferry.
- Can you get there and back in a day?
- How much luggage do you have to carry?

Accommodation
- How close to the meeting place do you have to be (10 mins or 1 hr)?
- Do the four of you have to be together?
- Will you only need bed & breakfast?
- Is accommodation required before or after the presentation?

(21)

SCOPING MEASURES

EXAMPLE (Cont'd)

Continuing our example of the visit to Brussels, let's analyse time factors versus cost factors:

TIME

HIGH

Walk/bike Car/ferry
B&B (1 hr away)

Car/ferry with overnight stop
5 star hotel (1 hr away)

Train (2nd class)
B&B (5 mins away)

Train (1st class)/plane
5 star hotel (5 mins away)

LOW

HIGH

COST

SPONSORS & END-USERS

As much information as possible should be gathered about the wants and concerns of the sponsors and end-users. A helpful way to remember how to identify the channels of influence that may exist on a project is to apply the **DRUGS** test:

D ecider   Authorises and initiates project and agrees the terms of reference.

R ecommender   Wants change and needs to be convinced it is an integral part of the business. Projects always have friends and enemies. Ensure this person is on your side!

U ser   Implements, and influences Recommender.

G atekeeper   Experts who are listened to by Decider and secretaries/personal assistants who can limit or extend access to Decider/Recommender.

S takeholders   Can be outside the project entirely (eg: legal, moral and ethical third parties).

In a small project, the Recommender and the User could be the same person, such as an area retail manager who is changing the monthly reporting of sales from the five shops in her area.

FORCE-FIELD ANALYSIS

This tool works where there is a 'thorny' topic or a politically sensitive issue to resolve such as changes to work patterns or financial packages or wholesale changes to reporting structures which may involve management and workers needing to negotiate changes. You will need to resolve the weight of the forces favouring and resisting the change.

The key is to ensure that the size of the arrows is commensurate with the weight you give to that issue. Some arrows cancel themselves out and, therefore, leave you with a balance of probabilities as to whether you will be able to implement the change envisaged. At least you will be going in with your eyes open!

FORCE-FIELD ANALYSIS CHART

When scoping a project you will often encounter uncertainty or conflict: do we do this or that? It may be necessary to have a mechanism for sorting out which stakeholder or sponsor takes priority. Where a decision is difficult to make, because the pros and cons are too many and complex to weigh up in your mind, try applying **this** chart. The example below is to help decide whether to upgrade a computer system at work. The longer the arrow, the greater the influence it exerts. In which direction is the force stronger?

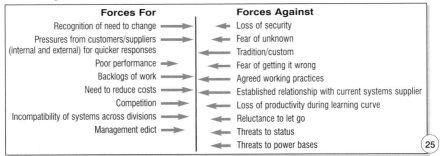

Forces For	Forces Against
Recognition of need to change ⟶	⟵ Loss of security
Pressures from customers/suppliers (internal and external) for quicker responses ⟶	⟵ Fear of unknown
	⟵ Tradition/custom
Poor performance ⟶	⟵ Fear of getting it wrong
Backlogs of work ⟶	⟵ Agreed working practices
Need to reduce costs ⟶	⟵ Established relationship with current systems supplier
Competition ⟶	⟵ Loss of productivity during learning curve
Incompatibility of systems across divisions ⟶	⟵ Reluctance to let go
Management edict ⟶	⟵ Threats to status
	⟵ Threats to power bases

ESSENTIALS OF COMMUNICATION

Gathering information from sponsors, end-users and other involved parties is all about communication. So when you're planning a discussion, **POURS** before you decide:

P lan	What to tell and ask
O utline your understanding	Clarify objectives and seek constant feedback
U se open questions	5Ws 1H (as illustrated)
R eflect	Use closed questions for confirmation (you have two ears and one mouth and should use them in that proportion)
S ummarise	Agree actions

INFORMATION GATHERING

When scoping the project, the nature of the information required falls into four categories:

1. Time   How much time? How urgent is urgent? What will happen if the status quo is maintained?

2. Cost   How much money do you need? How much will be saved by changing the procedure?

3. Quality   To what standard must the outcome be measured?

4. Quantity   How many? What will happen if quality is sacrificed for quantity?

All four categories must be balanced against each other. As with all projects, sacrifices must be made to achieve the objective. The secret is to ensure that the project sponsors have weighed up the options that the project team has put to them.

SCOPING THE PROJECT

INFORMATION GATHERING

 1. TIME

Having defined your desired outcome, consider the questions you may need to ask in order to obtain the relevant information about the impact of time within the project:

Q How much time is available?

Q How much time does each key activity need?

Q How urgent is urgent?

Q What will happen if the status quo is maintained?

Q Why will the change make such a difference to the speed of information delivery or response time to a customer?

Q Within what degree of accuracy should completion of the project take place? Are we talking days, hours or minutes?

Q Does any stage or activity of the project have a particular deadline or restriction on time?

Q Do different time zones have to be co-ordinated?

Q How much notice do contractors or suppliers need?

Q What activities can take place in parallel rather than in series?

INFORMATION GATHERING

 COST

You may need to ask the following:

Q What is the budget?

Q Are there penalty clauses that could be imposed? (Construction projects – eg: motorways - are notorious for completing late and over-budget unless penalty clauses are included in the original project specification.)

Q Is there funding up front or is it 'pay as you go' or cash on delivery of the system or product change? (How is cashflow affected?)

Q What will it cost?

Q What will it save over the longer term?

Q Are 'guesstimates' acceptable for some decisions?

Q Is this a 'fixed-cost' or a 'cost-plus' project?

Q What detail of record-keeping is required to reclaim costs?

Q Is there discount for bulk?

INFORMATION GATHERING

 QUALITY

You may need to ask the following:

Q What are the expressed outcomes to be measured?

Q Who is measuring and do they know what they are measuring?

Q Who is responsible for quality?

Q When do you check for quality: at the input stage, on-going or when the project is finished?

Q Are you expecting 'zero defects'? What tolerance levels are acceptable?

Q What is the procedure when quality is below acceptable levels?

Q What steps or procedures could be put in place to ensure quality at every stage?

Q Is functionality more important than cosmetics?

INFORMATION GATHERING
|||| QUANTITY

The following quantity-related questions may be relevant:
- **Q** How much can be produced without sacrificing quality for quantity?
- **Q** At what level of output do 'economies of scale' come into effect?
- **Q** How many people do you need?
- **Q** How long do you need them for?
- **Q** How much scope is there for 'wastage' or 'trial and error'?
- **Q** Does everyone need their own desk, computer, phone, etc?
- **Q** What's the likelihood of spares being needed?
- **Q** How much of x can we hold in stock?
- **Q** What is the turnover of staff or materials?
- **Q** Can we cope with the demand, usage, etc?

TERMS OF REFERENCE

The terms of reference for a project are an outcome of scoping, and should be agreed before the planning stage gets underway. They should be documented and should constitute a contract between the sponsor/end-user and the project team. They should always contain:

1. Objectives and outcomes

2. Project sponsor (see DRUGS)

3. Customers or beneficiaries

4. Scope - what's in and what's left out (assumptions)

5. Budget/resources

6. Time-scales/milestones

7. Risks

8. Who is doing what for whom? (Roles and responsibilities must be defined with a job specification so no one overlaps or encroaches on another's territory.)

SCOPING YOURSELF & THE PROJECT TEAM

In a project you will need to manage the people as well as the task. Achieving the balance will require tact and diplomacy, and not a little good fortune!

- **A people-orientated approach** requires available time to allow for everyone to participate, and for team members to navigate the learning curve which often dictates the pace of the project. This approach can inspire commitment to change and team loyalty.

- **A task-orientated approach** puts the needs of the project before those of the people, and is generally adopted where deadlines are tight. Unfortunately, as sponsors invariably want things yesterday, more and more unrealistic or compromising deadlines are set, so this becomes the norm. Loyalty and commitment are difficult to attain and crisis management may be called for.

You may not get to choose but, if you do, try to put people first. And if you can, choose the right people, as the next page indicates.

SCOPING THE PROJECT TEAM

Research by Professor Belbin shows that each individual of every team is different and, therefore, people with the same skills working on a project may behave differently. Their behaviours will affect you whether you are the project's sponsor, leader or team member. Below, we use Belbin team styles to define the roles that people have natural tendencies to play in project teams, notwithstanding the functional skills and knowledge they bring:

Co-ordinator	Clarifies goals and promotes participative decision-making but could delegate the 'walking of the talk'	**Resource investigator**	Will find out how other teams make it work but will tend to lose enthusiasm once planning stage is over
Shaper	Challenging, will drive through change but will expect everyone to change behaviour immediately	**Team worker**	Will diplomatically encourage and support others but may avoid conflict at the expense of the project
Implementer	Will turn ideas into practical actions (or scoping into plans) but may be inflexible about outcomes created by others	**Monitor evaluator**	Will see all the options and watch for milestones but may lack the drive to inspire others
Plant	Will be creative and unorthodox in approach but may ignore how the plan should be implemented	**Completer finisher**	Will want the change delivered on time but will want to do it all him/herself and will worry about the outcomes unduly

SCOPING YOURSELF

Before embarking on the project, it is helpful to recognise what it is that you and others on the team bring to the project. This could identify any gaps that need filling and reinforce the team spirit and self-belief. Useful questions to ask are:

Q What skills do you have?

Q What relevant knowledge do you possess?

Q What did you learn last time? Write it down!

Q Is this a secondment or are you just doing two jobs that are both full-time?

Q What do you want to get out of the project?

Q Who will carry out your appraisal?

Q How will your line boss know if you have a problem or know about your success?

Q Who cares for the needs of fellow project team members?

Q In what situations do you work best?

> *"Change is something the top asks the middle to do to the bottom,"*
> **Rosabeth Moss Kanter**

DETERMINING THE RIGHT AGENDA

To help confirm the scope of the project, you should know the answers to these
questions before you begin the planning:

- Who does your solution need to perform for?
- Q What results and benefits should the solution produce?
- Q What costs or penalties do you want to avoid?
- Q What limitations and restrictions apply?
- Q What do you want to happen?
- Q What don't you want to happen?

• DRUGS & POURS

ON
D ANALYSIS

IT WHEEL
MS
ODEL

CONSIDER OPTIONS
• 5 M ANALYSIS
• 5 Cs OF
  DECISION-MAKING
• GANTT CHARTS
• PERT DIAGRAMS

PLANNING THE PROJECT

PROJECT MANAGEMENT CYCLE: STEP 2

As we have shown in the previous chapter, there is a lot of essential information to collect and assimilate before you can even contemplate putting together a plan. If you don't know where you are heading, how can you possibly know how to get there!

Planning will involve:

- **Considering options**
  - generating ideas and opinions
  - assessing your 5 M resources
  - using the 5 Cs of decision-making

- **Recording the plan**
  - applying charts and graphs

CONSIDERING OPTIONS

The 5 Cs of decision-making is a useful reminder of the process ahead of implementation:

Consider
- clarify the nature of the project, time and other constraints
- ask yourself and others what information you need
- **identify objectives**

Consult
- gather the maximum amount of information available
- call a meeting of those involved or their representatives
- **brainstorm** if necessary
- decide at which point the consultation will stop

Crunch
- review all the options and **take decision**
- write down your implementation plan

Communicate
- provide briefings on what will happen, why, and who the decision affects
- back-up briefing with written confirmation of the decision
- make sure everyone understands when the decision will be implemented

Check
- check that the briefing is carried out
- run spot checks to monitor effectiveness
- review the impact of the decision and **take any corrective action**

RECORDING THE PLAN

Plans should be
drawn up for the following:

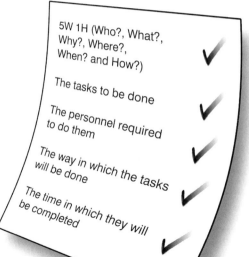

5W 1H (Who?, What?,
Why?, Where?,
When? and How?) ✓

The tasks to be done ✓

The personnel required
to do them ✓

The way in which the tasks
will be done ✓

The time in which they will
be completed ✓

TEAM FRAMEWORK

Whether or not you were able to choose your team, as discussed under 'Scoping', getting their contributions to the planning of the project is another good opportunity for team-building. After all, plans should not be drawn up in isolation. The following are key questions that need to be asked of, and answered by, new teams:

- What makes a good team?
  - key skills (Belbin team roles)
  - effective procedures
  - stages of development and application of SWOT

- How can our team work smarter?
  - for each other
  - for their stakeholders

- How can the team identify milestones to measure and review their success en route?

- How can the team communicate more effectively...
  - with the leader?
  - among themselves?
  - with their stakeholders?

- How can the team use their human resources more effectively?

- How can the team be effectively managed?

- How will the team appraise themselves/be appraised?

(41)

PROJECT TEAM ISSUES

When you assemble your team at the outset of a project, be sure to address with them:

- Why they are here — mission

- What they will be doing — goals

- How they will recognise progress — planning the milestones, communication and feedback

- What's in it for them — recognition

- What happens when they need help — support

Ensure you get the right mix of traits, not just skills (see page 34).

PLANNING THE PROJECT

5 M ANALYSIS

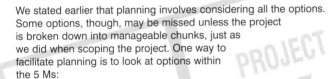

We stated earlier that planning involves considering all the options. Some options, though, may be missed unless the project is broken down into manageable chunks, just as we did when scoping the project. One way to facilitate planning is to look at options within the 5 Ms:

- Machinery
- Manpower
- Materials
- Methods
- Money

5 M ANALYSIS

Difficulty (Problem/Obstacle)	Machinery	Manpower	Materials	Methods	Money
1					
2					
3					
4					
5					

PLANNING THE PROJECT

5 M ANALYSIS

MACHINERY

🅠 What PCs or tools are required?

🅠 What vehicles, rooms, chairs, tables, wipe boards, etc, are required to fulfil the project?

MANPOWER

🅠 What people resources will be required?

🅠 For how long?

🅠 How will their appraisal be conducted?

🅠 How will they be managed?

🅠 What skills do they have/lack?

🅠 What training programme needs to be undertaken to develop the users and project members?

🅠 Should they read this pocketbook before starting the project?

5 M ANALYSIS

MATERIALS

Q What raw materials are required?

Q Where can we get these materials?

Q Is it worth spending more to get materials that are more durable, easier to maintain, more portable, etc?

Q Will the new materials require changes to systems, special skills, etc?

Q Will the materials be available at the appropriate time and in the right quantity?

METHODS

Q What methods will be used as the 'language' around which all project discussions take place (eg: Gantt charts)?

Q How will information be reported back to the project team and end-users?

Q What will be the reporting lines to the project manager – daily, weekly, monthly?

Q How much information needs to be reported?

Q What marketing methods are required? (It may be necessary to draw up a marketing plan to sell the concept of the project, either internally or externally.)

5 M ANALYSIS

MONEY

Q What financial resources are required to fulfil the objective?

Q What budget has been allocated?

Q What cost savings have been projected?

Q What will be the short-term cost to 'prime the pump'; to get the project off the ground?

Q What will be the impact of the project on cashflow?

PLANNING THE PROJECT

5 M ANALYSIS
EXAMPLE

In this example the team project is to move a company of 60 people to the other side of the city. By applying the 5 M analysis, the following considerations are highlighted:

MACHINERY

- What size of removal vehicles is required? How many of each?
- Is there a need for specialist equipment to remove fixed items or to transport heavy items indoors?

MANPOWER

- Are internal or external resources to be used?
- Will a removal company be engaged to remove all of the equipment and furniture? Or will a combination of internal and external resources be better?
- Will it be necessary to get assistance from telephone suppliers with phone/fax/PC cabling?
- What further help will be required?

5 M ANALYSIS

EXAMPLE (Cont'd)

MATERIALS
- Do we have the crates, cartons, etc, to pack the items for removal?
- What items actually have to be removed?
- What new materials will we require (eg: cabling and power sockets, new carpeting)?

METHODS
- Could greater use of a cheaper resource save the need for a more costly one?
- Does it make more sense for parts of the company to move first, or for everyone to move at the same time?

MONEY
- How much money is available to move the people and their equipment?
- Will the people who are moving actually conduct the move, ie: will they need to hire vans and will they be able to move the PCs and other items?
- What happens if there are breakages or C drives are damaged in the move?
- What about 'damage-to-goods-in-transit' insurance?

PROJECT MANAGEMENT TOOLS

Take care, it is easy to get bogged down in the mechanics of planning a project.

There are excellent software tools such as Microsoft Project or Suretrak which allow you to plan to any level of detail, but beware:

- A plan is a statement of intent not a destination in itself (as we move through different examples, see which tool suits your project best)

- However, a plan is important but it can be changed as the situation changes

GENERATING OPTIONS

The following shows a questioning approach which will bring out a number of options for incorporating into your plan:

Question	Style	Focuses on
What new ideas are triggered by imagining the ideal solution?	Visioning	• Goal • 'New' change
What new ideas result from adapting/improving what we already have?	Modifying	• What's working and not working • Incremental change
What new ideas are generated by combining existing elements to form a new solution?	Experimenting	• People and processes • Incremental change
What new ideas result from changing our assumptions?	Exploring	• Beliefs and assumptions • 'New' change

THE HOCKEY STICK EFFECT

You will always need more resources up to and just after the change you introduce. This is when you need to hold your nerve, as people and resources will be at their tightest and you will be under intense pressure to release people. Don't plan any holiday at this time; plan some before the major change — and three months after to recover!

THE HOCKEY STICK EFFECT

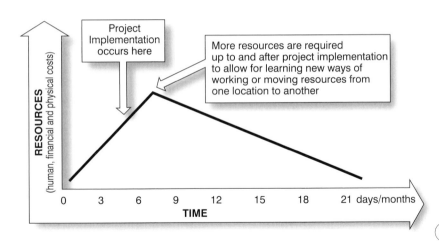

Project Implementation occurs here

More resources are required up to and after project implementation to allow for learning new ways of working or moving resources from one location to another

RESOURCES (human, financial and physical costs)

0   3   6   9   12   15   18   21 days/months

TIME

TASK OR PROJECT?

When is an undertaking an everyday management task and when is it a project? Perhaps the answer lies in the distinction we make when thinking about such issues.

When we have a defined plan, procedure or organisational system, and clear channels of communication, all of which have been in place for some time, we are **unconsciously skilled**.

However, when a project manager/leader performs tasks that are unfamiliar, undefined or uncertain, and the lines of communication are unknown, he or she will need to be **consciously skilled**.

The role of planning in project management is to make things certain, defined and clear when communicating - and create ***order out of chaos!***

The following page gives a clearer view of the key differences between task and project.

TASK OR PROJECT?

The differences between everyday management tasks and project management are:

Issue	Everyday Task	Project
Undertaking:	Familiar	Unfamiliar
Staff:	Known	Temporary
Team roles:	Established	Uncertain
Relationships:	Co-operation	Negotiable
Authority:	Clear position	Little/indirect
Information source:	Routine	New/uncertain
Attitude to change:	Desirable	Essential
Momentum:	Maintained by system	Threatened by system
Time-scales:	Extended/long-term	Ring-fenced/finite
Co-ordination:	Hierarchical	Network/matrix

GANTT CHARTS

Of all the project management tools this is probably the simplest to understand, the easiest to use and the most comprehensive. It allows you to predict the outcomes of time, cost, quality and quantity and then come back to the beginning.

It helps you to think about people, resources, dates, overlaps and key elements of the project, and you can concertina 10 separate Gantt charts into one overall chart.

A Gantt chart is a horizontal bar chart that graphically displays the time relationship of the steps in a project. It is named after Henry Gantt, the industrial engineer who introduced the procedure in the early 1900s. Each step of a project is represented by a line placed on a chart in the time period when it is to be undertaken. When completed, the Gantt chart shows the flow of activities in sequence as well as those that can be underway at the same time.

To create a Gantt chart, list the steps required to complete a project and estimate the time required for each step. Then list the steps down the left side of the chart and time intervals along the bottom. Draw a line across the chart for each step, starting at the planned beginning date and ending at the completion date of that step.

GANTT CHARTS

Some parallel steps can be carried out at the same time with one taking longer than the other. This allows some flexibility for the start of the shorter step, as long as the plan has it finished in time to follow in subsequent steps. This situation can be shown with a dotted line continuing on to the line when the step must be completed.

When the Gantt chart is finished, you will be able to see the minimum total of time for the project, the proper sequence of steps and which steps can be underway at the same time.

You can add to the usefulness of a Gantt chart by also charting actual progress. This is usually done by drawing a line in a different colour below the original line to show the actual beginning and ending dates of each step. This allows you to quickly assess whether or not the project is on schedule.

Gantt charts are limited in their ability to show the interdependencies of activities. In projects where the steps flow in a simple sequence of events, they can portray adequate information for project management. However, when several steps are underway at the same time and a high level of interdependency exists among the various steps, PERT diagrams (discussed later) are a better choice.

GANTT CHARTS

EXAMPLE

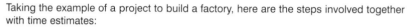

Taking the example of a project to build a factory, here are the steps involved together with time estimates:

Project steps	Days	Project steps	Days
1. Draw working plans	15	10. Install heating/air conditioning	5
2. Obtain building permit	16	11. Insulate	5
3. Form/ pour foundation	5	12. Install plasterboard	5
4. Frame walls and roof	5	13. Install interior doors and trim	5
5. Install roofing	5	14. Paint interior	3
6. Install windows	1	15. Install electrical fixtures	2
7. Install exterior cladding	10	16. Clean up	3
8. Paint exterior	3	17. Install floor covering	2
9. Install electrical wiring	10	18. Hand over to client (ceremony)	1
		Project duration	**101**

GANTT CHARTS

EXAMPLE (Cont'd)

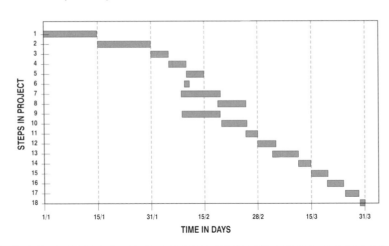

PERT DIAGRAMS

PERT stands for **P**rogramme **E**valuation and **R**eview **T**echnique. For planning purposes it is more sophisticated than Gantt charts, as it is appropriate for projects with many steps.

In a PERT diagram: events are represented by circles or other convenient, closed figures; activities are represented by arrows connecting the circles; and non-activities connecting two events are shown as dotted-line arrows. A non-activity represents a dependency between two events for which no work is required (lapsed time).

☐	**EVENT**
▬	**ACTIVITY**
▬	**NON ACTIVITY/** **LAPSED TIME**

PERT diagrams are most useful if they show (on the activity line) the time schedule for completing an activity. Time is recorded in a unit appropriate for the project, with days being most common and hours, weeks or even months being occasionally used. Some diagrams show two numbers for time estimates - a high estimate and a low estimate.

The most sophisticated PERT diagrams are drawn on a time scale, with the horizontal projection of connecting arrows drawn to represent the amount of time required for that particular activity. This can incorporate slack time in the project.

PERT DIAGRAMS

To draw a PERT diagram, list the steps required to finish a project and estimate the time required to complete each step. Then draw a network of relationships among the steps, keeping in mind the importance of proper sequencing. The number of the step from your list is written in the appropriate event circle to identify that step. The time to complete the following step is shown on the arrow. Steps that can be underway at the same time are shown on different paths. Be sure to include all distinguishable steps.

A PERT diagram not only shows the relationship among various steps in a project, but also serves as an easy way to calculate the critical path. The critical path is the longest path through the network and as such identifies essential steps that must be completed on time to avoid delay in completing the project. The critical path is shown as a solid line in the example that follows.

The usefulness of a PERT diagram can be increased by colouring each step as it is completed. Actual time can be written over the estimated time to maintain a running tally of actual versus planned time along a critical path. This makes it a useful tool for evaluation purposes later.

PLANNING THE PROJECT

PERT DIAGRAMS

EXAMPLE

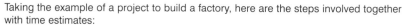

Taking the example of a project to build a factory, here are the steps involved together with time estimates:

Project steps	Days
1. Project started	-
2. Working plans completed	15
3. Building permit obtained	16
4. Foundation poured	5
5. Walls/ roof framed	5
6. Roofing completed	5
7. Windows installed	1
8. Exterior cladding installed	10
9. Exterior painted	3
10. Wiring in	10

Project steps	Days
11. Heating/air conditioning in	5
12. Insulation completed	5
13. Plasterboard hung	5
14. Interior doors/trim installed	5
15. Interior painted	3
16. Interior fixtures installed	2
17. Clean-up completed	3
18. Floor covering installed	2
19. Project completed	-
Project duration	**100**

PLANNING THE PROJECT

PERT DIAGRAMS
EXAMPLE (Cont'd)

Numbers in the circles correspond to the
steps listed on the previous page.
Numbers on the lines show the
days required to complete the
following step.

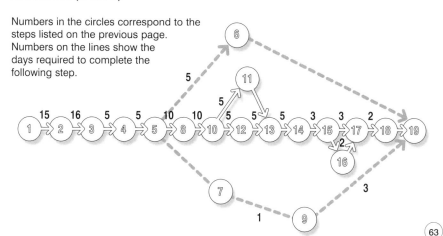

PROBLEM IDENTIFICATION

Applying the Pareto principle can indicate where the effort for change is best concentrated.

- Wilfredo Pareto discovered that 80% of the wealth of Italy was owned by 20% of the people.

- Many people use the same 80:20 principle to concentrate on eliminating 80% of the defects/problems that will occur in 20% of the business process. By continuously striving to record the errors it is generally accepted that most of the work problems will be overcome. Remember, in any project the goal only stays visible if the team concentrate on the top 20% of the problems that account for 80% of the solution.

ALLOWING FOR MILESTONES

When scoping the project we talked about the importance of measurable outcomes. The plan must be geared towards achievement of all outcomes, with milestones identified en route to keep you on track. Don't leave the measurement until it's too late to adjust!

"What gets measured gets done", Tom Peters

Some notable 'faux pas' include:

- **The development of a tolling system for cars wanting to enter Singapore city:** devised by a firm from another country, where motorists drive on the right-hand side, the toll booths are located in the wrong place. Consequently, drivers have to lean over the passenger side of the vehicle or get out to reach the booth!

- **A new rail network in the UK:** the new trains purchased were not of the right gauge for the track.

Don't take all you are told at face value - always check with a third party.

NOTES

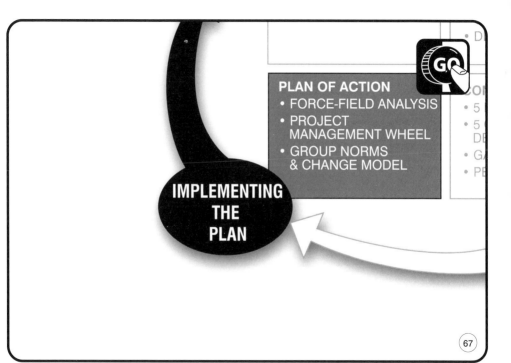

PLAN OF ACTION
- FORCE-FIELD ANALYSIS
- PROJECT MANAGEMENT WHEEL
- GROUP NORMS & CHANGE MODEL

IMPLEMENTING THE PLAN

PROJECT MANAGEMENT CYCLE: STEP 3

Planning the work is one thing; working the plan is another. The trick is to keep as close to the original plan as possible, assuming, of course, that it was put together along the scoping guidelines of Chapter 3.

Implementing actions will involve:

● Applying the plan and working with team members and end-users

● Monitoring at check points (milestones) to make sure that the objective is being achieved

● Resolving problems as they occur (plans can change and may be permitted to go off track to a certain extent, as long as the objective is achieved by the end)

CONTROL POINT IDENTIFICATION CHARTS

Implementation should focus on the achievement of agreed outcomes, so that if a problem is encountered with the plan, other courses of action can be employed. Use the framework shown right to explore and record the need for contingencies, so that you are ready if they are needed.

Hindsight will teach you that you underestimated the resources required, so always include contingency in your demands for money, manpower, etc.

Control element	What is likely to go wrong?	How and when will I know?	What will I do about it?
Quality			
Cost			
Time			
Quantity			

TEAM CULTURES

Understanding the culture of the organisation, and that of the project team, can have a significant impact on the success of implementing plans.

Where would your organisation culture feature on this chart?

Organisation culture	Closed	Part open	Fully open
GOALS	are announced	are communicated	are agreed on
INFORMATION	is a status symbol	traded with like goods	exists in abundance
MOTIVATION	is manipulative	focused on the needs of the staff	has identification as its goal
DECISIONS	are only taken from above	partly delegated	fall on staff level
MISTAKES	are only made by staff	responsibility taken for	can be made
CONFLICTS	are unwelcome	are mastered	represent chances for innovation
CONTROL	comes from above	is partly delegated	self-control
MANAGERIAL STYLE	authoritarian, patriarchal	co-operative	ad hoc
AUTHORITY	wants obedience	wants co-operation	wants partnership
MANAGER	absolute ruler	problem-solver, decision-maker	strategist for change

THE PARTICIPATIVE APPROACH

Participation means:

- Deciding with…
- Implementing with…
- Acting with...
- Reviewing with...
    - ….line management

RISK-TAKING

Risk is the father of innovation.

For innovation to succeed there must be **RISK:**

R elationships within the team

I nformation shared between each other

S upport from the project leader

K indness to listen to the ideas of each other, often at a time when you are working intensely and don't feel like it!

PARTICIPATION

Seek participation in the formation of strategic goals - get opinion formers on your side!

- Conduct a one-hour training session on the subject of understanding change, so that attendees see the value of participation
- Soft issues are important to most businesses, and performance of people matters
- Change is about hearts and minds
- Look at issues as a process, not which department should do what!
- Hierarchies should be unimportant; there may be too much to do to allow a 'tell' culture to exist
- Rivalry is unimportant and disappears when the team work together to achieve the end goal

IMPLEMENTING THE PLAN

COLLECTIVE DECISION-MAKING

Project teams should take collective decisions and implement them by taking
responsibility for their actions.

- Decisions need to be taken collectively so that you can be sure you are all saying
  the same thing no matter which forum (eg: training courses on management of
  change, team-building and technical cross-skilling courses) you are addressing
- This also applies to departmental team meetings, site presentations, corporate core
  team briefings, etc
- Encourage contributions of articles in all forms of corporate communications
  (eg: house magazines) so that the project is not seen as a faceless wonder
- Decision-makers must be accountable for the successful implementation of their
  decision
- When implementing, be the eyes and ears for the whole project team; remember to
  report back all the information gained - unfiltered and without any political
  'flavouring' either
- Take feedback on a variety of project issues; relay it to the appropriate area and
  ensure that remedial action is taken where required
- Assume nothing

VALUE OF WORKSHOPS

Here is an example of a project in which the management structure of the organisation was radically changed:

Team leader workshops were held. These included sessions on the vision of the future and were run by the project team members with open debates as to what the vision should look like.

Business planning sessions were also run by a line manager and trainer to explain the theory of flatter structures. All the team leaders each had 16 team members reporting to them, requiring them to appraise and empower a diverse team, many of whose skills were unknown to the leader.

Where new skills were identified as being relevant to the business, but were not in place, then training was provided. By demonstrating the value of the workshops to senior management, the very best HR practices were accepted.

PROGRESS REPORTING

Keeping everyone informed of progress to date is a necessary activity of implementing. The purpose of reporting back is to highlight events significantly different from expectations rather than provide a diary account of all the period's happenings.

- For weekly/monthly progress reports use the **KISS** technique: **K**eep **I**t **S**hort and **S**imple

- Include bad news. Reports only need to state what has changed and what has been achieved. This is sometimes known as exception reporting.

- One-to-one progress meetings are useful for project members to iron out micro issues (strategic issues should be left to the group meetings).

- Group project meetings should be held once a week face-to-face. An example for a meeting agenda is shown here.

AGENDA
(5 mins per team member)

Personnel
Training
Premises
IT
Branches rolling out phase by phase
Operations and methods
Implementation team
Meeting critique (5 mins)

Rotating chair and secretary
Meeting max 50 mins

KEEP COMMUNICATION VISIBLE!

Many companies who have now restructured branch service networks, have decided to use wallboards with an electronic display to show how often and how quickly the phones are being answered. Outstanding work by the back office teams is also recorded, on whiteboards.

It is important to site these boards so that all members of the team, as well as visiting clients and customers, can see that service is important. Project teams really want the changes to be visible, practical, everyday enhancements to real-life work.

Everyone should be involved in discussing the best visible places as a project group. Each team should make its own choice, pointing out the pros and cons and overcoming objections such as 'big brother is watching you'. Any changes made by the implementation team should be introduced as a branch benefit rather than as a threat.

Each member of the team should be responsible for implementing a part of the project whether on site or across functional boundaries. This will ensure that the project team is accountable!

FEEDBACK

HELPER is a simple process for providing feedback:

H ear each member's contribution
E laborate with additional positive examples
L ook at all members' ideas for improvement
P romote additional suggestions for improvement
E mpower the team: don't dictate
R ecognise overall positive behaviours, results and contributions

DESIGN & BUILD

Keeping control of the key outcomes of the project is only possible when the designer actually implements the plan. The 'design & build' technique works because the project team understand the constraints (site, organisation, available resources) and formulate their plan accordingly. Pragmatic, perhaps, but there are benefits as these examples demonstrate:

- It is said that Christopher Wren was present throughout the construction of St. Paul's Cathedral in London. He did not let the builders change his specification without recourse to him.

- In a major new London hospital, expensive porter trolleys that moved patients from the accident and emergency department to the operating theatre were too wide for the corridor doors. It was discovered later that no one had thought to check the specifications with the porters, even though the administration, medical and technical teams had all been consulted. If one trolley had been walked through, the problem could have been identified and resolved with little time and cost (see 'milestones' in the previous chapter). As it was, it became a toss up as to whether it was cheaper to change the trolleys or the doors!

PROVIDING TRAINING & SUPPORT

> *"In a changing world some things remain the same ... cock-ups."*
> **Anon.**

It is essential that attention is given to the education and training of all who may be affected by the project, not just those who are directly working on it.

- Use attitude surveys to get a 'fix' on current attitudes and to identify where the focus of the education (and perhaps even of the project) may be needed
- Provide timetables, Gantt charts and other support material to keep everyone with you

IMPLEMENTING THE PLAN

THE CHANGE PROCESS

The implementation phase of some projects may take months, or even years.

Those experiencing the change process may even include you, but most certainly will include those who are likely to undergo upheaval, anxiety and uncertainty because of the project outcome. Such people need to be allowed the opportunity to express where they are and to have their concerns addressed. See 'Sell the benefits' in the final chapter.

An adaptation of Elizabeth Kubler-Ross's bereavement counselling model provides the language which the people in an organisation can use to identify where they are with the change. There are four stages:

Denial

Resistance

Exploration

Commitment

THE CHANGE PROCESS
 DENIAL

- This can be explained as the ostrich phase or the bad dream: "I will wake up tomorrow and this will all have been a bad dream". Change is painful to all; it's just a matter of degree.

- It can be expressed in physical, emotional, logical and highly illogical ways to others: "The company will see the error of its ways. We will stop this working. It is impossible to run the department/branch without me. Other companies tried all these changes and found they did not work. Why do we always follow the failures of old, clapped-out theory?".

These outbursts, which will be familiar to many, are examples of what is said once the change is announced.

THE CHANGE PROCESS
 RESISTANCE

- This is the guerrilla warfare phase when we all feel like rebelling. We are outside our comfort zone and lash out at all people, things, views and ideas with which we feel uncomfortable.

- We hear things like: "Why me? Why must I change? No research has been done." All the anger that is felt by the individual or their peer group comes to the surface, if the organisation allows it to. It is critically important to allow this to happen. As someone once said, "Let the bad out so that the good may come in".

- If the lid is held down the consequences will be more disastrous, as the staff that remain after the changes will be looking to sabotage the change. This applies to all levels of the company, up to the boardroom.

THE CHANGE PROCESS

SAYING GOODBYE TO THE PAST (BRIDGE TO STAGE 3)

- At some time there is a letting go, saying goodbye to the past. While not forgetting, people may forgive or, at least, understand the reasons why the structural changes had to be made.

- In bereavement terms, this could be seen as a wake. One organisation encouraged and paid for a good party before a new amalgamated branch was opened, so there was a clear break in time. It allowed the staff to, quite literally, 'let their hair down'. The staff and management were told that this was a part of the change process and that this was why it was being held. Openness again is a crucial part of the new organisation.

- Communicating with all people all of the time cannot be underestimated. As with justice, it must not only be done, but it must be seen to be done.

- Evidence of showing a degree of humanity during the process destroys the platform for the negative opinion formers.

THE CHANGE PROCESS

EXPLORATION

- Once people feel that the worst is over there is a period of adjustment. This is when the questions emerge. These could be asked in a variety of contexts and venues. Informally, questions may arise by the coffee machine, in the restaurant, canteen or lift, during shared bus or car journeys, on the e-mail or telephone or, most commonly, at the work desk. Since informal contact is as important as the formal team briefing or line management communication, it too needs to be managed.

- We will believe or disbelieve what we hear, depending upon the regard we have for the communicator.

- Time must be given to answering the questions, however ridiculous, as little if any work will be done until the information is given. 'Walking the talk' is essential.

THE CHANGE PROCESS

 COMMITMENT/ACCEPTANCE

- There is now an acknowledgement that things have changed and working the new system is here to stay
- It does not necessarily mean unbridled enthusiasm
- The days of resisting and wanting to sabotage the change are over

GROUP NORMS

Theory has it that any group (work-based or otherwise) will follow four stages of development:

Forming   The group first gets together with its common aim.

Storming   A short while after the group forms, aims and objectives are questioned and the group experiences conflict from within.

Norming   Because of the conflict, policy and procedures are drawn up and agreed by the consensus of the group.

Performing   The group adheres to the policy and procedures and works effectively towards its aim.

You can expect your own project team to pass through these stages though, with foresight, you can be prepared and control what is controllable!

GROUP NORMS

THE CHANGE MODEL

Simply by overlaying the stages of group development onto the change process grid, we can see that when we undergo change it has the same effect as making us start again. Effective project management should, therefore, involve facilitating the transition of those affected by the change.

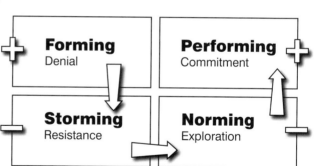

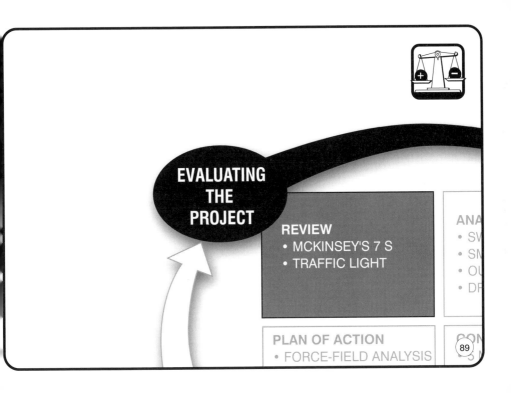

EVALUATING THE PROJECT

REVIEW
- MCKINSEY'S 7 S
- TRAFFIC LIGHT

ANA
- SW
- SM
- OU
- DR

PLAN OF ACTION
- FORCE-FIELD ANALYSIS

CON
- S M

PROJECT MANAGEMENT CYCLE: STEP 4

The act of reviewing the plan really begins during the implementation phase, but at the end of the project we also want to look at the lessons to be learned from how it was carried out, and to see whether its completion has had the desired effect.

There are several ways to review a project:

1. McKinsey's 7 S model of change
2. Questioning (What went well? What did not go well? What should we change?)
3. Traffic light technique

EVALUATING THE PROJECT

MCKINSEY'S 7 S MODEL

Consider the impact of change upon these 7 Ss (we are looking at this after the project, but the same model could be used at the planning stage):

Strategy   The vision and business plan - is there a new direction and a need to replan?

Systems   Computer and manual processes - are we more efficient; where can we improve?

Staff   The affected parties - are they familiar with the changes and have they accepted them?

Skills   Future knowledge and skills needed - what are the training or recruitment implications?

Style   Methods of communication - are there fewer misunderstandings; has technology gone too far?

Shared values   Culture and ethos - are we contradicting or losing sight of who we are?

Structure   Reporting lines and framework - is decision-making enhanced and duplication of effort avoided?

Are there other issues to be addressed now?

QUESTIONING/TRAFFIC LIGHT TECHNIQUE

Ask yourself, the team and the project sponsor:

- What went well in the project?
- What did not go well in the project?
- What would we change for the next project?
- What was missing, or missed but not foreseen?

Alternatively, apply the traffic light technique:

Red - What should we stop doing?

Amber - What do we need to consider continuing with or perhaps stopping?

Green - What did we do well that should be imparted to others?

EVALUATING THE PROJECT

PROJECT MANAGEMENT TOOLS

The very tools that formed the basis of the project plans now become the basis for review. Typically, these would be:

- Gantt
- SWOT
- PERT
- Pareto
- Control point identification charts

All have been discussed in earlier chapters. How accurate did they prove to be and where could changes be made for the future?

NOTES

PROJECTING
WITH PEOPLE

DAY ONE AS A NEW PROJECT MANAGER

- Ensure all of your team have a desk, or at least a phone/fax/e-mail point
- Tell each member of the team that he or she must buddy up with another member to ensure there is always cover in case of emergency or illness (the show must go on!)
- No one is bigger than the project; each team member must be prepared to do the good and the bad to get the job done
- All team members must identify what they want from the project (what their personal objectives are) and should share this with the team to ensure there is no favouritism and to avoid giving rise to feelings that some members are carrying the rest of the team

PROJECT MANAGER

THINGS TO BE AWARE OF IN ANY PROJECT

'Scope creep'. Recognise that every piece of work you are getting is a potential project and that people not directly affected by the project will want you to add things to it. Check with the sponsor before proceeding!

Poor organisation of resources. Where team members work in disparate locations, communication problems can arise. There is no substitute for face-to-face meetings as they avoid misunderstandings; this is especially crucial at the start of a project.

Lack of role definition for team members. Clearly defining who does what and who is responsible for what is critical.

Dependency on one person. Each member of the team must be able to double up for other team members to ensure the project is not dependent on one person.

Unclear objectives. Ensure you have agreed objectives with the sponsor of the project. If there are any material changes ensure that these are agreed and the specification is altered. You can always change a plan but ensure that there is one.

Incomplete plan. Ensure every part of a plan is written down to avoid argument.

Project funding. Know who holds the purse strings as there will always be a trade off between time and cost.

PROJECTING WITH PEOPLE

ADVICE TO A NEW PROJECT LEADER

✔ Keep all informed
✔ Agree time-scales and double them!
✔ Allow for contingencies in the planning stage (eg: holidays and delays in the decision-making process of the project's decider/sponsor)
✔ Use IT tools (eg: Microsoft Project)
✔ Ensure your objectives are clear and check outcomes required!
✔ Be tenacious and trust the skills of the team
✔ Sell to and influence anyone who will help you (politics)
✔ Practise using tools (eg: Gantt and PERT) on everyday jobs at home and at work

✔ Get 'enough' research done - probably 80% will be enough

✔ Always consider the 'neighbours' - just as you would if any building work affected them - since change usually involves politics

SELL THE BENEFITS

"It is easier for the losers to see what they will lose than the gainers to see how they will gain."
Machiavelli

✔ Concentrate on selling the project to people, particularly those it will affect

✔ Sell the benefits in terms of what it will do for them:
  - Will it save them time, effort, money, embarrassment and injury?
  - Will it enhance their skills?

✔ Arrange your audience into target groups so you can focus on the benefits they alone receive, whilst addressing their particular concerns

PROJECTING WITH PEOPLE

COMMUNICATION

- Do it with enthusiasm: "Nothing great was ever achieved without enthusiasm", Emerson

- One manager described his day as "a series of five minutes for each of my team"; he has 100!

- Find a genuine reason to build self-esteem by describing in factual terms what you saw, heard, touched, smelt, tasted (eg: "You have written a good proposal for action by writing a structured, clear, concise report, with a conclusion that demands action. However, what about including the following points?" Or, "How could you improve this still further?")

- Always describe what you saw not how you felt; identify the evidence to support what you are saying? ('Gut feel' will never win friends for the long-term)

- In successful project teams: everyone contributes; everyone listens; everyone is courteous; everyone tells the truth; everyone is supportive

- You will only succeed if you communicate again and again and again ! check

- Remember the need to be fair, honest and confidential, either as an implementer or as a survivor

IMPACT OF A PROJECT ON YOU

- Project management normally means radical change for all involved including those making the changes
- The process affects each person in a different way
- Paternalism may give way to self-interest
- There is no magic formula to change management but there are things to avoid
- Perception is more important than reality
- Functional thinking is slow and departments or branches will only communicate from the top down or to a fellow worker if they are of the same grade
- Ideas get balked at constantly and 'steady as she goes' become the watch words
- Everyone knows that something must be done but not me and not now!

MORALE : THE RIPPLE EFFECT

Why people need .   *Change*

Use **MORALE** to encourage and motivate staff going through change:

Myself   The best encouragement that you can give is your absolute undivided
              attention, your interest, your concentration.

Open   Communicate - a greeting, congratulations, a recommendation to someone
              else, a thank-you, etc.

Remember   People expect attention from you on returning from a trip to see a
              client/customer, on achieving a milestone, on doing overtime, etc.

Attention A small surprise will do: flowers, a card, a smile, 'thanks', the ubiquitous
              cream buns, a personal letter, a box of sweets/biscuits on return from
              holiday - all unexpected attention.

Listen   Never refuse attention when someone asks for it. Children expect it but as
              adults we have been taught rejection. So, if we ask for attention (yes, some
              of us will have needed courage even to ask) we really need it! Never refuse!

Esteem   If you flatter without honesty, neither you nor the receiver will feel good
              about it. Your body language, and that of your team member, will clearly
              show what a fake you are!

BEWARE TECHNOLOGY FOR TECHNOLOGY'S SAKE

- Question the benefits of any change – there is a common misconception that technology can solve any problem

- Technology can be effective when the end user has been sold the benefits or becomes part of the project team, and when adequate user training has been provided

- New technology is often unused or ignored because the benefits or appeal to ease of use have not been explained to the end-user

- Your job is to find and sell solutions and provide the service that goes with them; not just provide a product

PROJECTING WITH PEOPLE

THE 4 Ts

The 4 Ts of a project to consider as a leader:

Training   People must know how the new system operates.

Technology   It is there to add value and speed up boring and repetitive tasks. It is not there for its own sake!

Tenacity   The need to keep on keeping on. Any project will have its detractors; if you are in charge, understand that your drive and enthusiasm will be needed in abundance to see the project through to a successful conclusion. Only you can make it work!

Teamwork   Ensure that your team are with you. If they have concerns then sort these out otherwise nothing will get done. You will need to regularly talk to and walk around the team, no matter how dispersed they are.

ACTION PLANS

motivating people.

Show an interest in the people working with you on a project and they, in turn, will invest their interest in their work.

Use action plans, like the one shown here, to 'buy in' project members and for review purposes.

Three Month Action Plan

Name:

Team:

Direct Report:

I have set myself the following goals to achieve (these should be a mixture of business and personal):

Number	Goal (What?)	Action (What will I do?)	Time Scale (By when?)
1			
2			
3			
4			
5			
6			
7			
8			
9			
10			

PROJECTING WITH PEOPLE

PROJECT 'HIGHS' & 'LOWS'

Below are the responses of 20 project managers who were asked for their 'highs' and 'lows' when working on a project:

HIGHS

- Success at end
- Recognition
- Planning
- Discovering hidden talents
- Overcoming politics
- Clarifying objectives
- Taking calculated risks

- Letting go ... (after)
- Moving goal posts
- Outside environment changing
- Let down by team
- Computer corruption
- Delays outside our control

LOWS